LOL

The FUNNIEST JOKES EVER!

Silver Dolphin Books
An imprint of Printers Row Publishing Group
A division of Readerlink Distribution Services, LLC.
10350 Barnes Canyon Road, Suite 100, San Diego, CA
92121
www.silverdolphinbooks.com

Printers Row Publishing Group is a division of Readerlink Distribution Services, LLC.
Silver Dolphin Books is a registered trademark of Readerlink Distribution Services, LLC.

All notations of errors or omissions should be addressed to Silver Dolphin Books, Editorial Department, at the above address. All other correspondence (author inquiries, permissions) concerning the content of this book should be addressed to:
Hinkler Books Pty Ltd
45-55 Fairchild Street
Heatherton Victoria 3202 Australia
www.hinkler.com
Illustrated by Glen Singleton
Cover Design by Hinkler Studio

ISBN: 978-1-68412-591-3
Manufactured, printed, and assembled in Heshan, Guangdong, China.
First printing, February 2019. LP/02/19
23 22 21 20 19 1 2 3 4 5

Contents

ANIMALS

What do you get when you cross an elephant with a fish?

Swimming trunks!

What happened when the dog went to the flea circus?

He stole the show!

What did the dog say when he was attacked by a tiger?

Nothing, dogs can't talk.

How did the skunk call his mother?

On a smellular phone.

What do you get if you cross a cocker spaniel with a rooster and a poodle?

Cockerpoodledoo.

Why are four-legged animals bad dancers?

Because they have two left feet.

What do you call a woodpecker with no beak?

A headbanger.

Why did the crowd faint when the parrot started talking?

He had fowl breath!

What do you get when you cross a chicken and a caterpillar?

Drumsticks for everyone!

What do you call a lamb with a machine gun?

Lambo.

What do you get when you cross a high chair and a bird?

A stool pigeon.

What do cats put in soft drinks?

Mice cubes.

What's 150 feet long and jumps every ten seconds?

A dinosaur with the hiccups.

What do you call a camel with three humps?

Humphrey.

What do you call a penguin in the desert?

Lost.

What do you get if you sit under a cow?

A pat on the head.

What do you call a duck with fangs?

Count Quackula.

What did Mr. and Mrs. Chicken call their baby?

Egg.

What kind of tie do pigs wear?

A pigsty.

Why don't turkeys get invited to dinner parties?

Because they use fowl language.

Which side of the chicken has the most feathers?

The outside.

What did the duck say when she finished shopping?

Just put it on my bill.

What do frozen cows do?

They give ice cream.

What is a dog's favorite food?

Anything that is on your plate!

What did the hen say when she saw scrambled eggs?

What a crazy, mixed-up kid.

What do you get when you cross a rooster with a steer?

A cock-and-bull story.

Why did the cow jump over the moon?

Because the farmer had cold hands.

Why do mother kangaroos hate rainy days?

Because their kids have to play inside.

Why did the chicken cross the basketball court?

He heard the referee calling fowls.

What do you call an elephant in a telephone booth?

Stuck.

What do you call an elephant that never washes?

A smellyphant.

What do you give a nauseous elephant?

A very big paper bag.

What's black and very noisy?

A crow with a drum set.

Why do elephants live in the jungle?

Because they can't fit inside houses.

Why are elephants wrinkled all over?

Because they can't fit on an ironing board.

Why are skunks always arguing?

Because they like to make a big stink!

What do you call a cow riding a skateboard?

A cow-tastrophe waiting to happen.

What do you get if you cross a parrot with a shark?

An animal that talks your head off!

Why did the elephant paint the bottom of his feet yellow?

So he could hide upside down in mustard.

Did you ever find an elephant in mustard?

No.

It must work then!

What's black and white and eats like a horse?

A zebra.

What do get if you cross a centipede with a parrot?

A walkie-talkie.

Weeeeeeee

What did the snail say when he hitched a ride on the turtle's back?

Weeeeeeeeeeeeeeeeeeeeeee!!!!

What do you get if you cross a duck with a rooster?

A bird that wakes you up at the quack of dawn!

WAKEY WAKEY RISE and SHINE

Did you hear the one about the dog running ten miles to retrieve a stick?

It was pretty far-fetched.

What's black and white and black and white and black and white?

A penguin rolling down a hill!

What do dogs and trees have in common?

Bark!

What is white, fluffy, and lives in the jungle?

A meringue-utan!

What's bright orange and sounds like a parrot?

A carrot!

What's tall, hairy, lives in the Himalayas and does 500 sit-ups a day?

The abdominal snowman!

What is a slug?

A snail with a housing problem.

What do you get if you cross a skunk with a bear?

Winnie the Poo.

What's the difference between an elephant and a flea?

An elephant can have fleas but a flea can't have elephants.

Did you know it takes three sheep to make a sweater?

Hmmm. I didn't even know they could knit.

What would you do if a bull charged you?

Pay him cash.

What steps would you take if a bull chased you?

Big ones.

What happened to the dog that swallowed the watch?

He got ticks.

Why is the sky so high?

So birds won't bump their heads.

Why do giraffes have long necks?

Because their feet stink.

What has stripes and goes around and around?

A zebra on a merry-go-round.

Where do bees go when they're sick?

To the waspital!

How do you milk a mouse?

You can't, the bucket won't fit underneath!

What time is it when you see a crocodile?

Time to run.

What time is it when an elephant sits on your fence?

Time to get a new fence.

What's a shark's favorite candy?

Jawbreakers!

What do you call a baby whale?

A little squirt.

What are feathers good for?

Birds.

Why didn't the ostrich see his friend coming?

He had his head in the sand!

What animal drops from the clouds?

A raindeer.

Are you a vegetarian because you love animals?

No, because I don't like plants.

Why did they cross a homing pigeon with a parrot?

So if it got lost it could ask for directions.

What has four legs and goes "Boo"?

A cow with a cold.

What do you call fourteen rabbits hopping backwards?

A receding hareline.

Why do gorillas have big nostrils?

Because they have big fingers.

What do you call a fly with no wings?

A walk.

What do you get if you cross a chicken with a yo-yo?

A bird that lays the same egg three times!

When is it bad luck to see a black cat?

When you're a mouse.

What's black and white and goes around and around?

A penguin caught in a revolving door.

Why are elephants gray?

So you can tell them apart from canaries.

What do leopards say after lunch?

"That sure hit the spots!"

What did the canary say when she laid a square egg?

Ouch!

Better move to the other side of the street

Why did the dog cross the street?

To slobber on the other side.

What's the difference between a barking dog and an umbrella?

You can shut the umbrella up.

Why are dogs like hamburgers?

They're both sold by the pound.

What did the duck say to the comedian after the show?

You really quacked me up!

Why do birds fly south?

It's too far to walk!

What do you give a pig with a rash?

Oinkment!

Ten cats were on a boat, one jumped off, how many were left?

None, they were all copycats!

Why did the chicken cross the road?

To see the man laying bricks.

What's black and white and makes a terrible noise?

A penguin playing the bagpipes.

What's a pelican's favorite dish?

Anything that fits the bill.

What do you get when you cross an elephant with a sparrow?

Broken telephone poles everywhere.

Why did the grizzly refuse to go to the opera?

He found the music unBEARable!

Who went into the tiger's lair and came out alive?

The tiger.

How do you start a flea race?

One, Two, Flea, Go!

What do frogs order in restaurants?

French flies!

Why does a hummingbird hum?

It doesn't know the words!

Did you put the cat out?

I didn't know it was on fire!

How do you know that carrots are good for your eyesight?

Have you ever seen a rabbit wearing glasses?

The rabbit who wouldn't eat his carrots as a child...

What does a crab use to call someone?

A shellular phone!

What do you get when you mix ocean water in a cauldron?

The Atlantic Potion!

What do you call a sleeping bull?

A bulldozer!

What do you get when you cross a cat with a lemon?

A sour puss!

What kind of cat should you not play cards with?

A cheetah!

Hickory dickory dock,

Three mice ran up the clock,

The clock struck one,

But the other two got away with minor injuries.

What do you give a dog with a fever?

Mustard, it's the best thing for a hot dog!

Why do cows wear bells?

Because their horns don't work!

What is gray, has big ears, and a trunk?

A mouse going on vacation!

What did the porcupine say to the cactus?

Are you my mother?

What happened to the snake with a cold?

She adder viper nose.

How can you keep moles from digging up your yard?

Hide the shovel.

What's the difference between a unicorn and a lettuce?

One is a funny beast and the other a bunny feast.

What would you get if you crossed a chicken with a mild-mannered reporter?

Cluck Kent.

What did Tarzan say when he saw the elephants coming over the hill?

Here come the elephants over the hill.

What is brown, has a hump, and lives in the North Pole?

A very lost camel!

What do you call a group of boring, spotted dogs?

101 Dull-matians!

Why can't a leopard hide?

Because he's always spotted!

What did scientists say when they found bones on the moon?

The cow didn't make it!

What cat has eight legs?

An octopuss.

What kind of dog tells time?

A watchdog!

How do you stop a rhino from charging?

Take away its credit card!

What do you call a pony with a sore throat?

A little horse!

What's the difference between a piano and a fish?

You can tune a piano, but you can't tuna fish!

What do you do with a blue whale?

Try to cheer him up!

Where do sheep go to get haircuts?

To the baabaa shop!

What looks like half a cat?

The other half!

Why can't elephants ride tricycles?

They don't have thumbs to ring the bell!

How do you fit an elephant into a matchbox?

Take out the matches!

How do you fit a tiger into a matchbox?

Take out the elephant!

What is gray with sixteen wheels?

An elephant on roller skates!

WHAT WEIGHS 4 tons HAS 16 WHEELS AND IS EXTREMELY DANGEROUS?

Why shouldn't you ever make an elephant mad?

Because elephants never forget!

Why is a snail stronger than an elephant?

A snail carries its house, an elephant only carries his trunk!

Why is an elephant large, gray, and wrinkled?

Because if it was small, white, and smooth, it would be an aspirin!

What did one firefly say to the other before he left?

Bye! I'm glowing now!

Why was the father centipede so upset?

All of his kids needed new shoes!

2 million pairs of shoes!!

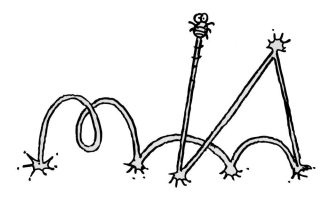

What do you call a mad flea?

A looney-tic!

What kinds of bees fight?

Rumblebees!

What are a bee's favorite soap operas?

"The Bold & The Bee-utiful" and "Days of our Hives"!

Why was the bee's hair sticky?

Because he used a honeycomb!

Why did the snail paint an S on its car?

So people would say, "Look at that S car go!"

What do you call two spiders who just got married?

Newlywebs!

If a snake and an undertaker got married, what would they put on their towels?

Hiss and Hearse!

What are six things smaller than an ant's mouth?

Six of its teeth!

How do bees travel?

They take the buzz!

How do you make a snake cry?

Take away its rattle!

Why did the firefly get bad grades in school?

He wasn't very bright!

What's worse than finding a worm in your apple?

Finding half a worm!

WHAT ARE YOU OUT HERE FOR?

PLAYING LOUD MUSIC

Where do you put a noisy dog?

In a barking lot!

Why did the fly land in the stick of butter?

He wanted to be a butterfly!

What do you call a fly when it retires?

A flew.

How can you tell an elephant from a banana?

Try to lift it up. If you can't, it's either an elephant or a very heavy banana.

What do you get when you cross an elephant with peanut butter?

Either an elephant that sticks to the roof of your mouth or peanut butter that never forgets.

What did the alien sheep say when they landed?

We come in fleece!

What do you call a monkey with a banana in each ear?

Anything, he can't hear you.

Why do tigers eat raw meat?

Because they can't cook.

Now you see it, now you don't, now you see it, now you don't. What is it?

A black cat on a zebra crossing.

What is big, green, and has a trunk?

An unripe elephant.

What happened when the cow jumped over the barbed wire fence?

It was an udder catastrophe!

What do you call an unmarried female moth?

Myth.

How does an elephant get down from a tree?

He sits on a leaf and waits for fall.

What do you get from nervous cows?

Milkshakes.

What do you get if you cross an alligator with a camera?

A snapshot.

Why do elephants' tusks stick out?

Because their parents can't afford braces!

What's the biggest moth in the world?

A mam-moth.

What's the biggest mouse in the world?

A hippopotamouse.

What's green, wiggly, and goes "hith"?

A snake with a lisp.

Why didn't the piglets listen to their father?

Because he was a boar.

Where can you buy ancient elephants?

At a mammoth sale.

Why did the lion spit out the clown?

Because he tasted funny.

What did the beaver say to the tree?

It's been nice gnawing you.

What college degree did the baboon get?

Monkey Business Administration!

What was the tortoise doing on the freeway?

About three miles an hour.

That's my funny bone!

How do you tell which end of a worm is the head?

Tickle him in the middle and watch where he smiles.

What do you give a sick bird?

Tweetment.

How do you stop an elephant from smelling?

Tie a knot in his trunk.

What has two legs and two tails?

A lizard flipping a coin.

How do you hire a horse?

Put four bricks under his feet.

What should you know if you want to be a lion tamer?

More than the lion.

Why did the fly *fly*?

Because the spider spied her.

What's bright blue and very heavy?

An elephant holding its breath.

What did the skunk say when the wind changed direction?

Ahhh, it's all coming back to me now.

Why did the viper vipe her nose?

Because the adder 'ad 'er 'ankerchief.

What's the best way to catch a rabbit?

Hide in the bushes and make a noise like lettuce.

What goes 'bonk' 99 times?

A centipede with a wooden leg.

Why do cows use the doorbell?

Because their horns don't work!

What's white on the outside, green on the inside, and hops?

A frog sandwich.

What does a porcupine have for lunch?

A hamburger with prickles.

What do get when you cross a dog and a cat?

An animal that chases itself.

GORILLA

RABBIT

How can you tell a rabbit from a gorilla?

A rabbit looks nothing like a gorilla.

What did the goose say when he got cold?

"I have people-bumps!"

What lies down a hundred feet in the air?

A centipede on its back.

What's the difference between a well-dressed man and a tired dog?

The man wears a suit, the dog just pants.

What lives at the bottom of the sea with a six-shooter?

Billy the Squid.

What did the mosquito say when he saw a camel's hump?

Gee, did I do that?

How many skunks does it take to stink up a room?

A phew.

How do goldfish go into business?

They start on a small scale.

Why do snakes have forked tongues?

Because they can't use chopsticks.

How do you spell "mousetrap" with three letters?

C-A-T.

What did the dog say when he sat on the sandpaper?

Rough, rough!

What is more fantastic than a talking dog?

A spelling bee!

What do you get if you cross a giraffe with a porcupine?

A 30-foot toothbrush.

What can go as fast as a racehorse?

The jockey!

If horses wear shoes, what do camels wear?

Desert boots.

Why don't kangaroos ride bicycles?

Because they don't have thumbs to ring the little bell.

What's the same size and shape as an elephant but weighs nothing?

An elephant's shadow.

What's black and white and hides in caves?

A zebra who owes money.

I'm staying right here until you come out with my $25

Where do you find a no-legged dog?

Right where you left it.

How do you get an elephant up an acorn tree?

Sit him on an acorn and wait twenty years.

What did one flea say to the other?

Should we walk or take the dog?

What did the cat have for breakfast?

Mice Krispies.

What goes tick, tick, woof?

A watchdog.

Why was the chicken sick?

Because it had people pox.

How do you get down from an elephant?

You don't get down from an elephant, you get down from a duck.

Why can't big cats be trusted?

They're often lion!

What's big, white, and furry, and found in outback Australia?

A very lost polar bear.

Why do horses only wear shoes?

Because they would look silly with socks on.

How do you stop a pig from smelling?

Put a cork in his nose.

What's the difference between an African elephant and an Indian elephant?

About 3,700 miles.

DINOSAURS

What do you get when you cross a dinosaur with a vampire?

A blood shortage.

I vant to sark your blurd...

What do dinosaurs put on their French fries?

Tomato-saurus.

What's extinct and works in rodeos?

Bronco-saurus.

What do you call a crying dinosaur?

A tear-odactyl!

What do you call a dinosaur with high heels?

My-feet-are-saurus.

What do you get if you give a dinosaur a pogo stick?

Big holes in your driveway.

What do you call a blind dinosaur?

Do-ya-think-he-saw-us?

What do you call a dinosaur that's a noisy sleeper?

Brontosnorus.

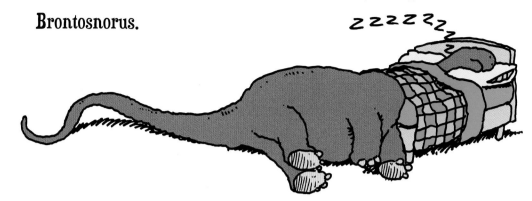

Why did the baby dinosaur get arrested?

He took the bus home!

What's the best way to call a *Tyrannosaurus rex*?

Long distance!

What does a *triceratops* sit on?

Its Tricera-bottom!

What do dinosaurs put on their floors?

Rep-tiles.

What dinosaur can't stay out in the rain?

Stegosaur-rust!

What do you call a group of people who dig for bones?

A skeleton crew.

What do you get when a dinosaur skydives?

A large hole.

What has a spiked tail, plates on its back, and wheels?

A *stegosaurus* on roller skates.

What's the difference between a dinosaur and a sandwich?

A sandwich doesn't weigh five tons.

What's worse than a *Tyrannosaurus* with a toothache?

A *diplodocus* with a sore throat!

Why couldn't the long-necked dinosaur see?

Because it had its head in the clouds!

What do you call a one-hundred-million-year-old dinosaur?

A fossil.

What do you get if you cross a dinosaur with a dog?

A very nervous mailperson.

What's the difference between dinosaurs and dragons?

Dinosaurs are still too young to smoke.

What did the egg say to the dinosaur?

You're egg-stinct.

Why didn't the dinosaur cross the road?

Because roads weren't invented.

What do you call a
scared Tyrannosaurus?

A nervous rex.

What dinosaur is home
on the range?

Tyrannosaurus Tex.

What do you call a dinosaur trained in martial arts?

A Tricera-chops!

What do you call a dinosaur eating a taco?

Tyrannosaurus Mex.

What do you call a dinosaur with magic powers?

Tyrannosaurus Hex.

What do you call a dinosaur that destroys everything in its path?

Tyrannosaurus Wrecks.

MISCELLANEOUS

Why is six scared of seven?

Because 7 ate 9.

What did the egg say to the whisk?

I know when I'm beaten.

Who's afraid of wolves and has a potty mouth?

Little Rude Riding Hood.

Why did the toilet paper roll down the hill?

To get to the bottom.

What's brown and sounds like a bell?

Dung.

Where are the Andes?

At the end of your armies.

What helps keep your teeth together?

Toothpaste.

What do you get if you cross a cowboy with a stew?

Hopalong Casserole.

What do you call a ship that lies on the bottom of the ocean and shakes?

A nervous WRECK!

How do you make a hotdog stand?

Steal its chair!

Why was Thomas Edison able to invent the light bulb?

Because he was very bright.

What's the best way to win a race?

Run faster than everyone else.

Can a match box?

No, but a tin can.

Why did the one-handed man cross the road?

He wanted to get to the secondhand shop!

During which battle was the knight killed?

His last one.

What did the floor say to the desk?

I can see your drawers.

What do you call someone who's run out of things to do in the ocean?

Surf-bored!

What was more useful than the invention of the first telephone?

The second telephone.

What's small, annoying, and really ugly?

I don't know, but it comes when I call my sister's name.

How do you use an Egyptian doorbell?

Toot-and-come-in.

What side of an apple is the left side?

The side that hasn't been eaten.

How can you tell a dogwood tree?

By its bark.

What invention allows you to see through walls?

A window.

What are the four letters the dentist says when a patient visits him?

ICDK (I see decay).

How did the dentist become a brain surgeon?

His drill slipped.

Why did the ballerina quit?

She didn't see the pointe in continuing!

Which months have 28 days?

All of them.

Miscellaneous

What's a plant's favorite song?

Twist and Sprout!

How do you make a fire with two sticks?

Make sure one of them is a match.

When do you put a frog in your sister's bed?

When you can't find a mouse.

Why did Polly put the kettle on?

She didn't have anything else to wear.

What did the little light bulb say to its Mom?

I love you watts and watts.

Why did the teacher wear dark glasses?

Because she had such a bright class.

Why do toadstools grow so close together?

They don't need mushroom.

What did the judge say to the dentist?

Do you swear to pull the tooth, the whole tooth, and nothing but the tooth?

What happens when the Queen burps?

She issues a royal pardon.

What did one wall say to the other wall?

I'll meet you at the corner.

Where did the king keep his armies?

In his sleevies.

Why was the math book sad?

Because it had so many problems.

What's the letter that ends everything?

The letter G.

What did the stamp say to the envelope?

Stick with me and we will go places.

You can say that again!

What do you call a man with an elephant on his head?

Squashed.

I have ten legs, twenty arms, and fifty-four feet. What am I?

A liar.

What did the tie say to the hat?

You go on ahead, I'll just hang around.

What do you call a
boomerang that doesn't
come back to you?

A stick.

Where was the Declaration
of Independence signed?

At the bottom.

Why does lightning shock
people?

It doesn't know how to
conduct itself.

What did the pencil sharpener say to the pencil?

Stop going in circles and get to the point!

Why do trains love food so much?

They love to chew-chew!

What do Alexander the Great and Kermit the Frog have in common?

They have the same middle name!

There are three kinds of people in the world: those who can count, and those who can't.

What's the easiest way to get on TV?

Sit on it.

What has four legs and doesn't walk?

A table.

Where do you find giant snails?

At the ends of their fingers.

Name three inventions that have helped humans get up in the world.

The elevator, the ladder, and the alarm clock.

What are brown, hairy, and have no legs but walk?

Dad's socks.

How do you saw the sea in half?

With a sea-saw.

What's easy to get into but hard to get out of?

Trouble.

Mom, why isn't my nose twelve inches long?

Because then it would be a foot.

Dad, can you see any change in me?

No, why, son?

Because I swallowed twenty cents.

How did the rocket lose his job?

He was fired.

What's yellow and wears a mask?

The Lone Banana.

Believe it or not... behind this mask, I'm really just an ordinary banana!

THAT'S IT... YOU'RE FIRED!

What has many rings but no fingers?

A telephone.

What do you get if you jump into the Red Sea?

Wet.

What's brown and sticky?

A stick.

What do you call a lazy toy?

An inaction figure.

Why did the balloon
burst?

Because it saw the soda pop!

What do all the Smiths
in the telephone book
have in common?

They all have telephones.

Why didn't the bird study
for the big test?

She decided to wing it!

What do you get if you cross the Atlantic with the *Titanic*?

About half way.

Why did the bacteria cross the microscope?

To get to the other slide.

What do you do if your nose goes on strike?

Picket.

What's the hardest part about sky diving?

The ground!

What's the difference between a TV and a newspaper?

Ever tried swatting a fly with a TV?

What did the little mountain say to the big mountain?

Hi, Cliff!

Why did the traffic light turn red?

You would too if you had to change in the middle of the street!

How much does it cost for a pirate to get earrings?

A buccaneer!

What is the difference between a jeweler and a jailer?

A jeweler sells watches and a jailer watches cells!

What did the digital clock say to its mother?

Look, Ma, no hands.

Why didn't the man die when he drank poison?

Because he was in the living room.

What do hippies do?

They hold up your leggies.

What did Snow White say while she waited for her photos?

Some day my prints will come!

What did one raindrop say to the other?

Two's company, three's a cloud.

What do you call a snowman with a suntan?

A puddle!

What did one penny say to the other penny?

We make perfect cents.

What did the Pacific Ocean say to the Atlantic Ocean?

Nothing. It just waved.

Who was the smallest man in the world?

The guard that fell asleep on his watch.

What can jump higher than a house?

Anything, houses can't jump!

Why did the bungee jumper take a vacation?

Because he was at the end of his rope.

Why did the frog have such big eyes?

Because he saw his phone bill.

What sort of star is dangerous?

A shooting star.

Why did the belt go to jail?

Because it held up a pair of pants.

What is the name of the detective who sings quietly to himself while solving crimes?

Sherlock Hums!

Why was the butcher worried?

His job was at steak!

What's the difference between an elephant and a matterbaby?

What's a matterbaby?

Nothing, but thanks for asking!

What did the shirt say to the blue jeans?

Meet you on the clothesline—that's where I hang out!

What did the big hand of the clock say to the little hand?

Got a minute?

What kind of music does your father like to sing?

Pop music.

What's the easiest way to find a tack in your carpet?

Walk around in your bare feet.

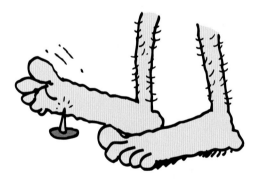

What did the parents say to their son who wanted to play drums?

Beat it!

Where do you find baby soldiers?

In the infantry.

Can February March?

No. But April May.

What's the definition of intense?

That's where campers sleep.

What do you call a man who stands around and makes faces all day?

A clockmaker.

What did one toilet say to the other toilet?

You look a little flushed!

Did you hear the one about the man who went into the cloning shop?

When he came out, he was beside himself!

What did the key say to the glue?

"Stick with me, I can open doors for you!"

When does B come after U?

When you take some of its honey!

Why was the archaeologist upset?

His job was in ruins!

Where does a sick ship go?

To the dock.

Did I tell you the joke about the high wall?

I'd better not, you might not get over it.

Where can you find robot clowns?

The Big Apple Circuits!

What did one ear say to the other ear?

Between you and me, we need a haircut.

What did the ear 'ear?

Only the nose knows.

What flowers grow under your nose?

Tulips.

Did you know that Davey Crockett had three ears?

A right ear, a left ear, and a wild frontier.

Why does the ocean roar?

You would too if you had crabs on your bottom.

What will go up a drainpipe down, but won't go down a drainpipe up?

An umbrella.

What would you call Superman if he lost all his powers?

Man.

What has a hundred legs but can't walk?

Fifty pairs of pants.

I have five noses, seven ears, and four mouths. What am I?

Very ugly.

What did one eye say to the other eye?

Something that smells has come between us.

MONSTERS

Little Monster: I hate my teacher's guts!

Mommy Monster: Then just eat around them!

What's green, sits in the corner, and cries?

The Incredible Sulk.

You wouldn't like me if I start to cry...

What's a vampire's favorite dog?

A bloodhound!

What do vampires cross the sea in?

Blood vessels.

Why didn't the alien have a birthday party?

He forgot to planet!

What did King Kong say when his sister had a baby?

Well, I'll be a monkey's uncle.

Why did the zombie decide to stay in his coffin?

He felt rotten.

What happened when the abominable snowman ate a spicy meal?

He melted.

What do you call a good-looking, kind, and considerate monster?

A complete failure.

Little Monster: Should I eat my fries with my fingers?

Mommy Monster: No, you should eat them separately!

Mom, everyone at school calls me a werewolf.

Ignore them and comb your face.

What do sea monsters eat for lunch?

Potato ships!

Why did the cyclops give up teaching?

Because he only had one pupil.

Why do witches fly on broomsticks?

Because it's better than walking.

Why did Dracula take some medicine?

To stop his coffin.

What do devils drink?

Demonade.

What don't zombies wear on boat trips?

Life jackets.

What do you call a sleeping monster who won't keep quiet?

Frankensnore.

What happened to Frankenstein's monster when he was caught speeding?

He was fined $50 and dismantled for six months.

How does a monster count to thirteen?

On his fingers.

What happened to the monster that took the five o'clock bus home?

He had to give it back.

What kind of cheese do monsters eat?

Monsterella!

What do you get when you cross a vampire and a snowman?

Frostbite!

Aww, Mom, I hate my B-Negative cold!

Mother vampire to son:

Hurry up and eat your breakfast before it clots.

What do you call a monster that was locked in the freezer overnight?

A cool ghoul!

What do you call a single vampire?

A bat-chelor.

What did the witch say to the vampire?

Get a life.

What do you get when you cross a skunk with Frankenstein?

Stinkenstein!

What do you call a ten-foot-tall monster?

Shorty!

What is a vampire's favorite kind of coffee?

De-coffin-ated!

Why do Martians make good gardeners?

They all have green thumbs!

What does a monster say when introduced?

Pleased to eat you.

What did the baby zombie want for his birthday?

A deady bear.

Why did the sea monster eat five ships carrying potatoes?

Beacause you can't eat just one potato ship.

Why doesn't anyone kiss vampires?

Because they have bat breath.

What do you think the tiniest vampire gets up to at night?

Your ankles.

Little bloodsucker

Why do ghosts go to parties?

To have a wail of a time.

Why aren't vampires welcome in blood banks?

Because they only make withdrawals.

Why do ghosts hate rain?

It dampens their spirits.

What time is it when a monster gets into your bed?

Time to get a new bed!

Why did they call the Cyclops a playboy?

Because he had an eye for the ladies!

What does a ghost have to get before he can scare anyone?

A haunting license.

What did one ghost say to the other?

Don't spook until you're spooken to!

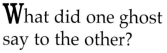

all I said was OOOOOOoHHHH

What do you call a witch that lives at the beach?

A sand witch!

How do you make a witch scratch?

Take away the *w*!

Why do mummies have trouble keeping friends?

They're too wrapped up in themselves.

What do you get when a ghost sits in a tree?

Petrified wood!

How many witches does it take to change a light bulb?

Just one, but she changes it into a toad!

Who is the best dancer at a monster party?

The Boogie Man!

Get down and booogie!

What is a monster's favorite drink?

Ghoul-Aid!

Where does a ghost go on Saturday nights?

Somewhere he can boogie!

What is a ghoul's favorite ride?

A roller-ghoster!

What is the difference between a huge, smelly monster and candy?

People like candy!

What is Dracula's favorite fruit?

Necktarines!

What is Dracula's favorite place in New York?

The Vampire State Building!

What is a ghost's favorite dessert?

Boo-berries and I Scream!

Why can't the Invisible Man pass school?

The teacher always marks him absent!

Why did the monster eat the North Pole?

He was in the mood for a frozen dinner!

Why are zombies so bad at hide-and-seek?

Their hiding spot it always a dead giveaway!

What is a ghost's favorite bedtime story?

Little Boo Peep!

What kind of mistake does a ghost make?

A boo-boo!

Why do they have a fence around the graveyard?

Everyone is dying to get in!

What is big, hairy, and bounces up and down?

A monster on a pogo stick!

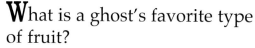

What is a ghost's favorite type of fruit?

Boo-berry!

What did the vampire say when he had bitten someone?

It's been nice gnawing you!

What did the skeleton say to the twin witches?

Which witch is which?

Why is the vampire so unpopular?

Because he is a pain in the neck!

What does a ghost do when he gets in a car?

Puts his sheet belt on!

Why didn't the ghost eat liver?

He didn't have the stomach for it!

What did the baby monster say to his babysitter?

I want my mummy!

What do you call five witches on a broom?

A carpool!

Why did Dr. Jekyll cross the road?

To get to the other Hyde!

What kind of fur do you get from a werewolf?

As fur away as you can get!

Who did the monster take to the Halloween dance?

His ghoul friend!

Why did Godzilla get a ticket?

He ran through a stomp sign!

What do you call a monster sleeping in a chandelier?

A light sleeper.

What is a mummy's favorite kind of music?

Rap!

What kind of boots do ghosts wear?

Ghoulashes!

Where do zombies live?

On dead ends!

Why are ghosts such terrible liars?

Because you can see right through them.

What is a ghoul's favorite food?

Monster mashed potatoes!

What do you call a dumb skeleton?

A numbskull.

What kind of witch turns out the lights?

A light switch!

What did one skeleton say to the other?

If we had any guts, we'd get out of here!

Why didn't the vampire dog win Best in Show?

Because he sucked!

How do you know when a ghost is sad?

He says Booooooooo Hoooooooo!

I hate those sad movies where the ghost gets exorcised.

What do you do with a green monster?

Put him in a paper bag till he ripens.

Did you hear about the ghost who ate all the Christmas decorations?

He got tinselitis.

What are ghosts favorite toys?

Scare bears!

What is Dracula's favorite ice cream flavor?

Vein-illa!

Why did the little monsters stay up all night?

They were studying for a blood test.

What do baby ghosts wear on their feet?

Booties!

Why did the troll tell jokes to the mirror?

He wanted to see it crack up!

Why do skeletons play the piano in church?

Because they don't have any organs!

How can you tell if a vampire has a cold?

He starts coffin!

What is a witch's favorite class in school?

Spelling!

What bear goes around scaring other animals?

Winnie the Boo!

What does a ghost read every day?

His horrorscope.

Where does Frankenstein's wife have her hair done?

At an ugly parlor.

What game do young ghosts love?

Hide and shriek.

How does an alien congratulate someone?

He gives him a high six.

How do monsters like their eggs?

Terrifried.

Why couldn't the skeleton go to the dance?

He had no body to go with.

Why didn't the skeleton cross the road?

Because he didn't have the guts to!

Why did it take the monster ten months to finish a book?

Because he wasn't very hungry.

How many vampires does it take to change a lightbulb?

None. They love the dark.

Why are skeletons
afraid of dogs?

Because dogs like bones.

What does a monster
eat after he's been to the
dentist?

The dentist.

Where do ghosts play golf?

At the golf corpse.

HA
HA
HA

What do you call the winner of
a monster beauty contest?

Ugly.

How do you make a skeleton
laugh?

Tickle his funnybone.

What do witches put in their
hair?

Scare spray.

Why are skeletons usually so calm?

Nothing gets under their skin!

What do ghosts eat for dinner?

Spook-etti.

Why don't skeletons wear shorts?

Because they have bony knees.

Do zombies have trouble getting dates?

No, they can usually dig someone up.

What does a boy monster do when a girl monster rolls her eyes at him?

He rolls them back to her.

What do you call a twenty ton two-headed monster?

Sir.

Doctor, Doctor, I have a hoarse throat.

The resemblance doesn't end there.

Doctor, Doctor, a bear ate the whole left side of my body!

You're going to be all right!

Doctor, Doctor, I feel like a tennis racket.

You must be too highly strung.

Doctor, Doctor, my nose is running.

You'd better tie it up then.

Doctor, Doctor, what is amnesia?

I don't know, I forgot!

Doctor, Doctor, I keep stealing things.

Take one of these pills, and if that doesn't work, bring me back a computer.

Doctor, Doctor, I feel like a pair of socks.

Well, I'll be darned.

Doctor, Doctor, I think I'm a video.

I thought I'd seen you before.

Doctor, Doctor I keep thinking I'm a yo-yo.

How are you feeling?

Oh, up and down.

Doctor, Doctor, how can I stop my nose from running?

Stick your foot out and trip it.

Doctor, Doctor, people keep disagreeing with me.

No, they don't.

Doctor, Doctor, I'm so ugly. What can I do about it?

Hire yourself out for Halloween parties.

Doctor, Doctor, I feel run down.

You should be more careful crossing the road then.

Now who didn't cross at the lights..?

Doctor, Doctor, I'm at death's door.

Don't worry, I'll pull you through.

Doctor, Doctor, my stomach is sore.

Stop your bellyaching.

Doctor, Doctor, I think I caught a cold!

Well, put it back!

Why do doctors wear masks?

Because if they make a mistake, the person won't know who did it!

Doctor, Doctor, I feel like a dog!

Then go see a vet!

Doctor, Doctor, I keep thinking I'm a doorknob.

Now, don't fly off the handle.

Doctor, Doctor, I'm a wrestler and I feel awful.

Get a grip!

Doctor, Doctor, some days I feel like a teepee, and other days I feel like a wigwam.

You're two tents.

Doctor, Doctor, I keep thinking I'm a dog.

How long has this been going on?

Ever since I was a pup.

Doctor, Doctor, everyone hates me.

Don't be silly, not everyone has met you yet.

Doctor, Doctor, I'm suffering from hallucinations.

I'm sure you are only imagining it.

Doctor, Doctor, I feel like a piano.

Wait a moment, while I make some notes.

Doctor, Doctor, will you treat me?

No, you'll have to pay like everybody else.

Doctor, Doctor, I keep thinking I'm a $10 bill.

Go shopping, the change will do you some good.

Doctor, Doctor, I swallowed a spoon.

Well, try to relax and don't stir.

oh...excuse me

Doctor, Doctor,
can you give me anything
for excessive wind?

Sure, here's a kite.

Doctor, Doctor, I swallowed
a roll of film.

Don't worry, nothing will develop.

Hey Doc...
I didn't swallow my kazoo...
...It was in my pocket all along!

Doctor, Doctor, I was playing a
kazoo and I swallowed it.

Lucky you weren't playing the
piano.

Doctor, Doctor, nobody ever
listens to me.

Next!

Doctor Doctor, I keep thinking I'm a joke.

Don't make me laugh.

Doctor Doctor, I'm turning into a trash can.

Don't talk rubbish.

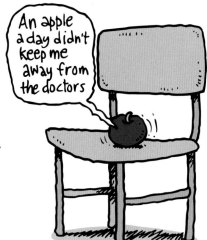

Doctor Doctor, I feel like an apple.

Well, don't worry, I won't bite.

Doctor, Doctor, I feel like a bell.

Well, take these, and if they don't work, give me a ring.

Doctor, Doctor, I'm as sick as a dog.

Well, I can't help you because I'm not a vet.

Doctor, Doctor, my eyesight is getting worse.

You're absolutely right, because this is a post office.

Doctor, Doctor, the first thirty minutes I'm up every morning I feel dizzy. What should I do?

Get up half an hour later.

Doctor, Doctor, what does this X-ray of my head show?

Unfortunately, nothing.

What medicine did the doctor give the pig?

Oinkment!

Doctor, Doctor, something is preying on my mind!

Don't worry, it will probably starve to death.

Doctor, Doctor, I feel like a set of curtains.

Well, pull yourself together.

Doctor, Doctor, I accidentally ate my pillow.

Don't be so down in the mouth.

Doctor, Doctor, I have a ringing in my ears!

Well, answer it.

Doctor, Doctor, every time I stand up I see visions of Mickey Mouse and Pluto, and every time I sit down I see Donald Duck!

How long have you been having these Disney spells?

Doctor, Doctor, it hurts when I do this!

Well, don't do that.

Doctor, Doctor, my leg hurts. What can I do?

Limp.

Doctor, Doctor, I snore so loudly I wake myself up!

Try sleeping in another room.

When do doctors get angry?

When they run out of patients.

I think it might be the bait you've eaten

What do you call a surgeon with eight arms?

A doctopus.

Why did the doctor tiptoe past the medicine cabinet?

Because she didn't want to wake the sleeping pills!

Doctor, Doctor, everyone thinks I'm a liar.

I don't believe you.

Doctor, Doctor, I feel like a pack of cards!

Sit down and I'll deal with you later!

Doctor, Doctor, I have a pain in the eye every time I drink hot chocolate!

Take the spoon out of your mug before you drink.

Doctor, Doctor, I only have 59 seconds to live!

Just a minute!

Doctor, Doctor, can you help me out?

Certainly—which way did you come in?

Doctor, Doctor, I dreamed that I ate a large marshmallow!

Did you wake up without a pillow?

Doctor, Doctor, I can't sleep at night!

Just lie on the end of your bed—you'll soon drop off.

Doctor, Doctor, I'm invisible!

I'm sorry, sir, I can't see you right now.

Doctor, Doctor, my sister thinks she's a squirrel!

Sounds like a nutcase to me.

Doctor, Doctor, I think I'm getting shorter!

You'll just have to be a little patient.

Doctor, Doctor, did you hear about the boy who swallowed a quarter?

No? Well, there's no change yet!

Doctor, Doctor, my son swallowed a pen. What should I do?

Use a pencil instead!

Doctor, Doctor, my wooden leg is giving me a lot of pain.

Why's that?

My wife keeps hitting me over the head with it!

Doctor, Doctor, my hair is falling out. Can you give me something to keep it in?

Yes, a paper bag.

What do doctors and teachers have in common?

They both like giving tests!

Doctor, Doctor, I haven't laughed in days!

You must have broken your funnybone!

Doctor, Doctor, I keep thinking I'm a dog.

Well, get up on this couch and I'll examine you.

I can't, I'm not allowed on the furniture.

Doctor, Doctor, can I get a second opinion?

Of course, come back tomorrow!

Doctor, Doctor, I feel like a window.

Where's the pane?

Doctor, Doctor, will my measles be better by next Monday?

I don't want to make any rash promises.

What did one tonsil say to the other tonsil?

Get dressed up, the doctor is taking us out!

Doctor, Doctor, I keep thinking I'm a fruitcake.

What's gotten into you?

Flour, raisins, and cherries.

Doctor, Doctor, you've got to help me, I keep thinking I'm a bridge.

What's come over you?

So far, a truck, a motorcycle, and two cars.

Doctor, Doctor, I keep hearing a ringing in my ears.

Where else did you expect to hear it?

Doctor, Doctor, what's good for biting fingernails?

Very sharp teeth.

FOOD

Waiter, you've got your thumb on my steak!

Well, I didn't want to drop it again.

Why don't eggs tell jokes?

They'd crack each other up!

What did the banana sitting in the sun say to the other banana sitting in the sun?

I don't know about you, but I'm starting to peel.

What do you call a fake noodle?

An impasta.

Waiter, there's a fly in my soup!

Don't worry, sir, the spider in your salad will get it!

What is a cannibal's favorite soup?

One with a lot of body.

What did the raspberry say to the other raspberry?

We shouldn't have got into this jam.

Waiter, what is this fly doing in my soup?

The backstroke, I believe.

How do you fix a broken pizza?

With tomato paste.

What's red, brown, and hairy?

Jelly toast dropped on the carpet.

What stays hot in the fridge?

Salsa.

How can you tell the difference between a can of soup and a can of baked beans?

Read the label.

What has bread on both sides and is afraid of everything?

A chicken sandwich.

Which nut is like a sneeze?

A cashew.

Hey! There's no chicken in this chicken potpie.

Well, do you expect to find dogs in dog biscuits?

Waiter, I'm in a hurry. Will my pizza be long?

No, it will be round.

Would Sir be requiring seafood tonight?

No...it gives me hives

Waiter, do you serve crabs in this restaurant?

Yes, sir, we serve anyone.

Waiter, this soup tastes funny.

Why aren't you laughing then?

Waiter, this apple pie is squashed.

Well, you told me to step on it because you were in a hurry.

Waiter, this egg is bad.

Well, don't blame me, I only laid the table.

Waiter, there is a small insect in my soup!

Sorry, sir, I'll get you a bigger one!

Why is a pea small and green?

If it was large and red, it would be a fire engine.

Where do bakers keep their dough?

In the bank.

Why did the potato cry?

Because the chips were down.

Waiter, there's a bug in my soup.

Be quiet, sir, or everyone will want one.

I'd like what he's having please.

Why did the baby cookie cry?

Because his mother was a wafer so long.

Waiter, do you have frog legs?

No, I've always walked like this.

The secret to making great wine...

dirty feet

What do you get when you step on a grape?

A little wine.

What did the teddy bear say when he was offered dessert?

No thanks, I'm stuffed!

NO!... not even a little mint

Have you heard the joke about the butter?

I'd better not tell you, you might spread it.

Two hot dogs are in a pan. One looks at the other and says, "Gosh, it's warm in here", and the other hot dog says,

Ahhr stop griping and just sizzle away quietly like the rest of us!

"GOODNESS GRACIOUS, IT'S A TALKING HOT DOG!"

Mom, can I have a dollar for the man who's crying in the park?

What's he crying about?

He's crying, "Hot dogs, one dollar."

What's the difference between pea soup and roast chicken?

Anyone can roast chicken.

Johnny, I think your dog likes me, he's been looking at me all night.

That's because you're eating out of his bowl.

What's long, green, and slowly turns red?

A cucumber holding its breath.

What do you make from baked beans and onions?

Tear gas.

Waiter, how long will my sausages be?

Oh, about 3 inches.

How do you fix a cracked pumpkin?

With a pumpkin patch!

Why was the fruit tree so famous?

It was kind of a fig deal!

Why did the jelly wobble?

Because it saw the apple turnover.

What is red and goes up and down?

A tomato in an elevator!

Why did the man at the orange juice factory lose his job?

He couldn't concentrate!

What did the veggie priest say to the congregation?

Lettuce pray.

Why are cooks mean?

Because they beat the eggs and whip the cream!

Why is a psychiatrist like a squirrel?

Because he's surrounded by nuts.

Why should you never tell secrets in a grocery store?

Because the corn has ears, potatoes have eyes, and beanstalk.

Waiter, bring me something to eat and make it snappy.

How about an alligator sandwich, sir?

Why did the cleaning woman quit?

Because grime doesn't pay.

Why did the raisin go out with the prune?

Because he couldn't find a date.

Why did Robin Hood rob the rich?

The poor didn't have any money.

What do you get if you cross a burglar with a cement mixer?

A hardened criminal.

If I had six grapefruit in one hand and seven in the other, what would I have?

Very big hands.

How do you make an egg roll?

Push it down a hill.

What did the cannibal have for breakfast?

Baked beings.

There goes your Father again!

POP CORN

What did the baby corn say to the mother corn?

"Where's pop corn?"

What did one plate say to the other plate?

"Lunch is on me!"

Why did the baker stop making donuts?

Because he was sick of the whole business.

GROSS

How do you make a
handkerchief dance?

Put some boogie into it.

What is the soft stuff between a
shark's teeth?

Slow swimmers.

Mommy, Mommy, can I lick the bowl?

No! You'll have to flush like everyone else.

Why are hot dogs so
bad-mannered?

They spit in the frying pan.

Why are basketball players never asked for dinner?

Because they're always dribbling!

What's the difference between a maggot and a cockroach?

Cockroaches crunch more when you eat them.

What's green, sticky, and smells like eucalyptus?

Koala vomit.

What do you get if you cross an elephant with a box of laxatives?

Out of the way.

Do you smell eucalyptus?

What is the difference between broccoli and boogers?

Kids don't like to eat broccoli!

Why did Piglet look in the toilet?

He was looking for Pooh.

What do you find up a clean nose?

Fingerprints.

What's invisible and smells like carrots?

Bunny farts!!

What's the last thing that goes through a bug's mind when he hits a car windshield?

His rear end.

What is a cannibal's favorite food?

Kidney beans!

How do you keep flies out of the kitchen?

Put a pile of manure in the living room!

What's the difference between a worm and an apple?

Have you ever tried worm pie?

How can you tell when a moth farts?

He flies straight for a second.

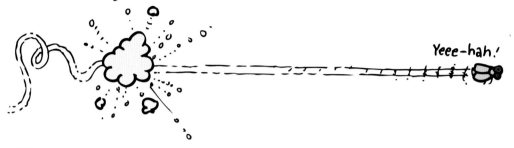

Yeee-hah!

What has two gray legs and two brown legs?

An elephant with diarrhea.

Why was the fish throwing up?

He was seasick!

What is worse than finding a maggot in your apple?

Finding half a maggot!

What's another name for a snail?

A booger with a crash helmet.

What's yellow and smells like bananas?

Monkey vomit.

What's green and red and goes 70 mph?

A frog in a blender.

What has fifty legs and can't walk?

Half a centipede.

WORLD LAND SPEED RECORD ATTEMPT

W hat's green and sings?

Elvis Parsley!

H ow did the doofus fall on the floor?

He tripped over the cordless phone!

W hy did the doofus break into two windows?

One to go in and the other to go out.

What's that on your shoulder?

A birthmark.

How long have you had it?...

What happened to the doofus who couldn't tell the difference between porridge and putty?

All his windows fell out.

What did the cat order at the Mexican restaurant?

A purrito!

Why did the doofus climb the glass wall?

To see what was on the other side!

Why did the doofus get fired from the banana factory?

He threw out all the bent ones.

Why was the doofus hitting his head against the wall?

Because it felt so good when he stopped!

How many fools does it take to screw in a light bulb?

Three . . . one to hold the bulb, and two to turn the chair!

How do you confuse a doofus?

Put him in a round room and tell him to sit in the corner!

How do you get a one-armed doofus out of a tree?

Wave to him.

What do you do if a doofus throws a hand grenade at you?

Pull the pin and throw it back.

Why did you tell everyone that I'm an idiot?

I'm sorry, I didn't know it was supposed to be a secret!

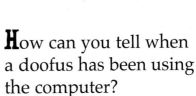

How can you tell when a doofus has been using the computer?

There is whiteout all over the screen!

What did the stupid burglar do when he saw his "WANTED" poster outside the police station?

He went in and applied for the job!

How do you keep a doofus in suspense?

I'll tell you tomorrow!

How did the doofus break his arm while raking leaves?

He fell out of the tree!

Why did the doofus get fired from the M&M factory?

Because he threw away all the W's!

Why did the doofus sleep under his car?

So he would wake up oily in the morning.

How do you sink a submarine full of fools?

Knock on the door.

Why was the fool's brain the size of a pea after exercising?

It swelled up!

What happened to the foolish tap dancer?

She fell in the sink.

Did you hear the one about the silly fox that got stuck in a trap?

She chewed off three legs and was still stuck.

Why was the doofus covered in bruises?

He started to walk through a revolving door and then changed his mind!

What is the difference between a doofus and a shopping cart?

Shopping carts have a mind of their own.

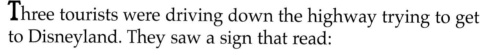

I'm going over here

Why did the doofus drive into the ditch?

Her turn signal was on.

Three tourists were driving down the highway trying to get to Disneyland. They saw a sign that read:

"Disneyland Left." So they went home.

How do you know if a doofus sent you an email?

There's a stamp on it.

Why did the Dalamation stop running?

He was starting to see spots.

Why did the doofus leap out of the window?

To try his new jumpsuit.

Why did the fool cross the road?

To get to the middle.

Why did the fool put a chicken in a hot bath?

So she would lay hard-boiled eggs.

How do you make a doofus laugh on a Sunday?

Tell him a joke on Saturday.

How can you tell when there's a doofus on a skyscraper?

When there's someone throwing bread to helicopters!

Why did the doofus buy a chess set?

He was saving it for a brainy day.

What did the foolish ghost do?

Climbed over walls.

What happened to the stupid jellyfish?

It set.

Stop! This is a one-way street!

Well, I'm only going one way!

Did you hear about the doofus who paid five dollars to have his thoughts read?

He got his money back.

What did the doofus call his pet zebra?

Spot.

Did you hear about the doofus who got a boomerang for his birthday?

He spent the next two days trying to throw the old one away.

Did you hear about the bungee jumper who shot up and down for 3 hours before they could bring him under control?

He had a yo-yo in his pocket!

What's red and hangs in an orange tree?

A silly strawberry.

SILLY INVENTIONS

An ejector seat on a helicopter.

A parachute that opens on impact.

Waterproof teabags.

You know... I've used this tea bag over 250 times... I think the secret's in the plastic coating.

A left-handed screwdriver.

A one-way staircase.

Knock-Knock.
Who's there?
Cargo.
Cargo who?

Car go beep beep!

Knock-Knock.
Who's there?
Alison.
Alison who?

Alison to the radio.

Knock-Knock.
Who's there?
Police.
Police who?

Police let me in.

COME ON...
OPEN UP....
this thing's heavy!

Knock-Knock.

Who's there?

Gotter.

Gotter who?

Gotter go to the toilet.

Knock-Knock.

Who's there?

Mister.

Mister who?

Mister last train home.

Knock-Knock.

Who's there?

My panther.

My panther who?

My panther falling down.

Knock-Knock.

Who's there?

Aardvark.

Aardvark who?

Aardvark a million miles for one of your smiles!

Knock-Knock.

Who's there?

Sue Prize.

Sue Prize, who?

Sue Prize for you! Happy Birthday!

Knock-Knock.

Who's there?

Norma Lee.

Norma Lee who?

Norma Lee I'd be at school, but I've got the day off.

Knock-Knock.

Who's there?

Gladys.

Gladys who?

Gladys Saturday, aren't you?

Knock-Knock.

Who's there?

Witches.

Witches who?

Witches the way home?

Knock-Knock.

Who's there?

Lettuce.

Lettuce who?

Lett-uce in, it's cold outside.

Knock-Knock.
Who's there?
Tank.
Tank who?

You're welcome.

Knock-Knock.
Who's there?
Turnip.
Turnip who?

Turnip for school tomorrow or there will be trouble.

Knock-Knock.
Who's there?
Sawyer.
Sawyer who?

Sawyer lights on, thought I'd drop by.

Knock-Knock.
Who's there?
Freeze.
Freeze who?

Freeze a jolly good fellow.

Knock-Knock.

Who's there?

Turnip.

Turnip who?

Turn up the heater, it's cold in here!

Knock-Knock.

Who's there?

Scott.

Scott who?

Scott nothing to do with you.

Knock-Knock.

Who's there?

Robin.

Robin who?

Robin you! So hand over your cash.

Knock-Knock.

Who's there?

Roach.

Roach who?

Roach you a letter, but I didn't send it.

Knock-Knock.

Who's there?

Nanna.

Nanna who?

Nanna your business.

There are hundreds of perfectly good banks to rob... ...so buzz off!

Knock-Knock.

Who's there?

Harley.

Harley who?

Harley see you anymore.

Knock-Knock.
Who's there?
Luke.
Luke who?

Luke through the peephole and you'll see.

Knock-Knock.
Who's there?
Boo.
Boo who?

What are you crying about?

Knock-Knock.
Who's there?
Eiffel.
Eiffel who?

Eiffel down.

Knock-Knock.
Who's there?
Justin.
Justin who?

Justin time for lunch.

Knock-Knock.
Who's there?
Nobel.
Nobel who?

No bell so I just knocked.

Knock-Knock.
Who's there?
Minnie.
Minnie who?

Minnie people would like to know.

Knock-Knock.
Who's there?
Troy.
Troy who?

Troy as I might, I can't reach the bell.

Knock-Knock.
Who's there?
Kenya.
Kenya who?

Kenya keep the noise down, some of us are trying to sleep.

Knock-Knock.
Who's there?
Iran.
Iran who?

Iran 25 laps around the track, and boy, am I tired!

Knock-Knock.

Who's there?

Avon.

Avon who?

Avon you to open the door.

Knock-Knock.

Who's there?

Lionel.

Lionel who?

Lionel bite you if you don't watch out.

Knock-Knock.

Who's there?

Cows.

Cows who?

No, cows moo!

Knock-Knock.

Who's there?

Border patrol.

Border patrol who?

We ask the questions here!

Knock-Knock.

Who's there?

Ice cream!

Ice cream who?

Ice cream, you scream!

Knock-Knock.

Who's there?

Miss Dee Buzz.

Miss Dee Buzz, who?

Miss Dee Buzz, can I get a ride with you?

Knock-Knock.

Who's there?

Iva.

Iva who?

Iva bone to pick with you!

Knock-Knock.

Who's there?

Shelby!

Shelby who?

Shelby comin' 'round the mountain when she comes!

Knock-Knock.

Who's there?

Dewayne!

Dewayne who?

Dewayne the bathtub before I drown!

Knock-Knock.

Who's there?

Midas.

Midas who?

Midas well let me in.

Knock-Knock.

Who's there?

Euripedes.

Euripedes who?

Euripedes pants, Eumenides pants.

Knock-Knock.

Who's there?

Miniature.

Miniature who?

Miniature let me in, I'll tell you.

Knock-Knock.

Who's there?

Arch!

Arch who?

Bless you!

Knock-Knock.

Who's there?

Max.

Max who?

Max no difference who it is—just open the door!

Knock-Knock.

Who's there?

Howard.

Howard who?

Howard I know?

Knock-Knock.

Who's there?

Red!

Red who?

Knock-Knock.

Who's there?

Red!

Red who?

Knock-Knock.

Who's there?

Red!

Red who?

Knock-Knock.

Who's there?

Red!

Red who?

Knock-Knock.

Who's there?

Orange!

Orange who?

Orange you glad I didn't say red?

Knock-Knock.

Who's there?

Little old lady.

Little old lady who?

I didn't know you could yodel!

Knock-Knock.

Who's there?

Artichokes.

Artichokes who?

Artichokes when he eats too fast!

Knock-Knock.

Who's there?

Letter.

Letter who?

Letter in or she'll knock the door down.

Knock-Knock.

Who's there?

Tuba.

Tuba who?

Tuba toothpaste.

Knock-Knock.

Who's there?

Phyllis.

Phyllis who?

Phyllis a glass of water, will you?

Knock-Knock.

Who's there?

Mikey.

Mikey, who?

Mikey won't work, did you change the locks?

Knock-Knock.

Who's there?

Avenue.

Avenue who?

Avenue heard these jokes before?

I'll come back again tomorrow...and the day after, too!

Knock-Knock.

Who's there?

Wayne.

Wayne who?

Wayne, wayne, go away, come again another day!

Knock-Knock.

Who's there?

Debate!

Debate who?

Debate goes on de hook if you want to catch de fish!

Knock-Knock.

Who's there?

Ben.

Ben who?

Ben knocking on the door all afternoon!

Knock-Knock.

Who's there?

Ammonia.

Ammonia who?

Ammonia little girl who can't reach the doorbell!

Knock-Knock.

Who's there?

Willube.

Willube who?

Willube my valentine?

Knock-Knock.

Who's there?

Water.

Water who?

Water friends for!

Knock-Knock.

Who's there?

William.

William who?

William mind your own business?

Knock-Knock.
Who's there?
S'more.
S'more who?

Can I have s'more marshmallows?

Knock-Knock.
Who's there?
Arncha.
Arncha who?

Arncha going to let me in? It's freezing out here!

Knock-Knock.
Who's there?
M-2.
M-2 who?

M-2 tired to knock!

Knock-Knock.
Who's there?
The Sultan.
The Sultan who?

The Sultan Pepper.

Knock-Knock.

Who's there?

Waiter.

Waiter who?

Waiter minute while I tie my shoe.

Knock-Knock.

Who's there?

Army.

Army who?

Army and you still friends?

Knock-Knock.

Who's there?

Wooden shoe.

Wooden shoe who?

Wooden shoe like to know.

Knock-Knock.

Who's there?

Wednesday.

Wednesday who?

Wednesday saints go marching in!

Knock-Knock.

Who's there?

Jamaica.

Jamaica who?

Jamaica mistake?

Knock-Knock.

Who's there?

Who.

Who who?

What are you—an owl?

Knock-Knock.

Who's there?

Ice cream soda.

Ice cream soda who?

Ice cream soda neighbors wake up!

Knock-Knock.

Who's there?

Shamp.

Shamp who?

Why, do I have lice?

Knock-Knock.

Who's there?

Augusta Wind.

Augusta Wind, who?

Augusta Wind blew my hat right off!

Knock-Knock.

Who's there?

Vitamin.

Vitamin who?

Vitamin for a party!

Knock-Knock.

Who's there?

Despair.

Despair who?

Despair tire is flat.

Knock-Knock.

Who's there?

Icon.

Icon who?

Icon tell you another knock-knock joke. Do you want me to?

Knock-Knock.

Who's there?

House.

House who?

House it going?

Knock-Knock.

Who's there?

Closure.

Closure who?

Closure mouth when you're eating!

Knock-Knock.

Who's there?

Icy.

Icy who?

I see your underwear.

Knock-Knock.

Who's there?

Wanda.

Wanda who?

Wanda see a movie later?

Knock-Knock.

Who's there?

Dishes.

Dishes who?

Dishes a very bad joke...!

Knock-Knock.

Who's there?

Weed.

Weed who?

Weed better mow the lawn before it gets too long.

C'mon baby don't break down on me now

Knock-Knock.

Who's there?

Alaska.

Alaska who?

Alaska one more time . . . let me in!

Knock-Knock.

Who's there?

Wooden shoe.

Wooden shoe, who?

Wooden shoe like to know!

Knock-Knock.

Who's there?

Cash

Cash who?

No thanks, but I'd love some peanuts!

Knock-Knock.

Who's there?

Howdy!

Howdy who?

Howdy do that?

Knock-Knock.

Who's there?

Leaf.

Leaf who?

Leaf me alone.

Knock-Knock.

Who's there?

Butcher.

Butcher who?

Butcher arms around me!

Knock-Knock.

Who's there?

Stopwatch.

Stopwatch who?

Stopwatch you're doing and open this door!!

Knock-Knock.

Who's there?

Winner.

Winner who?

Winner you gonna get this door fixed?

Knock-Knock.
Who's there?
Weirdo.
Weirdo who?

Weirdo you think you're going?

Knock-Knock.
Who's there?
Canoe.
Canoe who?

Canoe come out to play?

Knock-Knock.
Who's there?
Radio.
Radio who?

Radio not, here I come!

28...29...30.
Here I come!
Over and out...

RAIN TONIGHT

Knock-Knock.
Who's there?
Accordion.
Accordion who?

Accordion to the TV, it's going to rain tomorrow.

Knock-Knock.

Who's there?

Irish.

Irish who?

Irish I had a million dollars.

Knock-Knock.

Who's there?

Alex.

Alex who?

Alexplain later, just let me in.

Knock-Knock.

Who's there?

Zombies.

Zombies who?

Zombies make honey, zombies just buzz around.

Knock-Knock.

Who's there?

Cameron.

Cameron who?

Cameron a smile are all you need to take pictures.

Knock-Knock.

Who's there?

Abbot.

Abbot who?

Abbot you don't know who this is!

Knock-Knock.

Who's there?

Adore.

Adore who?

Adore is between us, open up!

Knock-Knock.

Who's there?

A king.

A king, who?

A king from head to toe after my workout!

Knock-Knock.

Who's there?

Alaska.

Alaska who?

Alaska no questions. You tella no lies.

Knock-Knock.
Who's there?
Irish stew.
Irish stew who?

Irish stew in the name of the law.

Knock-Knock.
Who's there?
Orson.
Orson who?

Orson cart!

Knock-Knock.
Who's there?
Felix.
Felix who?

Felix my ice cream, I'll lick his.

Knock-Knock.
Who's there?
Ice cream.
Ice cream, who?

Ice cream when I'm scared!

Knock-Knock.
Who's there?
Haywood, Hugh, and Harry.
Haywood, Hugh, and Harry who?

Haywood Hugh Harry up and open the door!

Knock-Knock.

Who's there?

Arthur.

Arthur who?

Arthur any more jelly beans in the jar?

Knock-Knock.

Who's there?

Theresa.

Theresa who?

Theresa green.

Knock-Knock.

Who's there?

Wilma.

Wilma who?

Wilma dinner be ready soon?

Change the channel on the TV, will you... my battery's dead again

Knock-Knock.
Who's there?
Abbott!
Abbott who?

Abbott time you opened this door!

Knock-Knock.
Who's there?
Oscar.
Oscar who?

Oscar silly question, get a silly answer.

Knock-Knock.
Who's there?
Sancho.
Sancho who?

Sancho a letter, but you never answered.

Knock-Knock.
Who's there?
Celia.
Celia who?

Celia later alligator.

Knock-Knock.
Who's there?
Betty.
Betty who?

Betty late than never.

Knock-Knock.

Who's there?

Snow.

Snow who?

Snow good asking me.

Knock-Knock.

Who's there?

Satin.

Satin who?

Who satin my chair?

Knock-Knock.

Who's there?

Barbie.

Barbie who?

Barbie Q.

Knock-Knock.

Who's there?

Carrie.

Carrie who?

Carrie me inside, I'm exhausted.

Knock-Knock.

Who's there?

Irish.

Irish who?

Irish I knew some more knock-knock jokes.

RIDDLES

What are two things you cannot have for breakfast?

Lunch and dinner.

Why did the boy throw butter out the window?

Because he wanted to see a butterfly!

What has eyes that cannot see, a tongue that cannot taste, and a soul that cannot die?

A shoe.

Who's that? It's me!

What can you hear, but not see, and only speaks when it is spoken to?

An echo.

What is there more of the less you see?

Darkness.

What ten letter word starts with gas?

A-U-T-O-M-O-B-I-L-E.

How many apples can you put in an empty box?

One. After that, it's not empty anymore.

When will water stop flowing downhill?

When it reaches the bottom.

What's black when clean and white when dirty?

A blackboard.

What's easier to give than receive?

Criticism.

If April showers bring May flowers, what do May flowers bring?

Pilgrims!

Where can you always find a helping hand?

At the end of your arm.

Why do firemen wear red suspenders?

To keep their pants up.

What kind of dress can never be worn?

Your address.

Can you give me a hand?

What weighs more—a pound of lead or a pound of feathers?

They both weigh the same.

What word is always spelled incorrectly?

Incorrectly.

What has a bottom at the top?

A leg.

Why is milk the fastest thing in the world?

Because it's pasteurized before you see it.

What kind of ring is always square?

A boxing ring!

What's the last thing you take off before bed?

Your feet off the floor.

What starts with an "e," ends with an "e," and only has 1 letter in it?

An envelope!

What is always coming but never arrives?

Tomorrow.

What did the piece of wood say to the drill?

You bore me.

What can you serve, but never eat?

A volleyball.

What do you put in a barrel to make it lighter?

A hole.

What stays in the corner and travels all around the world?

A postage stamp.

What do you call a bee that is always complaining?

A grumble bee!

What's taken before you get it?

Your picture.

Which room has no door, no windows, no floor, and no roof?

A mushroom!

What gets wet the more you dry?

A towel!

What's green, has four legs, and would kill you if it fell on you from out of a tree?

A pool table.

What washes up on very small beaches?

Microwaves!

What breaks when you say it?

Silence!

What gets bigger and bigger as you take more away from it?

A hole!

I can see CHINA..!!

What bow can't be tied?

A rainbow!

Why are false teeth like stars?

They come out at night.

Why do you go to bed?

Because the bed will not come to you.

What goes all around a pasture but never moves?

A fence!

What is H204?

Drinking!

What has teeth but cannot eat?

A comb!

What can you hold without touching?

Your breath.

What question can you never answer yes to?

Are you asleep?

What is the only true cure for dandruff?

Baldness!

What is big, red, and eats rocks?

A big, red, rock-eater!

What goes all over the world but doesn't move?

The highway!

What starts with a P, ends with an E, and has a million letters in it?

Post Office!

What is always behind the times?

The back of a watch.

Why can't it rain for two days in a row?

Because there is a night in between.

What goes up and does not come down?

Your age!

What was the highest mountain before Mt. Everest was discovered?

Mt. Everest.

What goes up and down but never moves?

A flight of stairs.

How many seconds are there in a year?

12 . . . 2nd of January, 2nd of February . . . !

Which candle burns longer–a red one or a green one?

Neither, they both burn shorter!

What runs across the floor without legs?

Water.

Which is the longest rope?

Europe!

What has holes and holds water?

A sponge.

Two coins add up to 30 cents. One of them is not a nickel. What are they?

A quarter and a nickel. One of them is not a nickel—but the other one is!

What runs but doesn't get anywhere?

A refrigerator.

What do you call a superb painting done by a rat?

A mouseterpiece!

What kind of ship never sinks?

Friendship!

What has four fingers and a thumb, but is not a hand?

A glove!

What cup can you never drink out of?

A hiccup.

What kind of coat can you put on only when it's wet?

A coat of paint.

What belongs to you but is used more by other people?

Your name.

Are you sure you want it in lime green, full gloss?

What kind of cup can't hold water?

A cupcake.

What weapon was most feared by medieval knights?

A can opener.

When things go wrong, what can you always count on?

Your fingers.

What flies around all day, but never goes anywhere?

A flag.

Where were potatoes first found?

In the ground.

What can you give away but also keep?

A cold.

What bet can never be won?

The alphabet.

What has two hands, no fingers, stands still, and runs?

A clock.

What is the beginning of eternity, the end of time, the beginning of every ending?

The letter "E."

How long should a person's legs be?

Long enough to reach their feet.

What can't walk, but can run?

A river.

When is it bad luck to be followed by a big black cat?

When you are a little gray mouse.

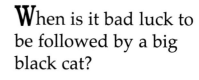

SPORTS

FOUR!

How many pairs of pants are you wearing?

Why did the golfer wear two pairs of pants?

In case he got a hole in one.

What does every winner lose in a race?

Their breath.

What do the losing team and scrambled eggs have in common?

They both get beaten.

What are the 4 seasons?

Baseball, basketball, soccer, and football!

What has 22 legs and two wings but can't fly?

A soccer team.

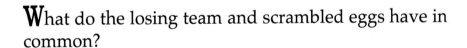

Where do old bowling balls end up?

In the gutter!

What illness do martial artists get?

Kung Flu.

What position did the pile of wood play on the football team?

De-fence!

When is a baby like a basketball player?

When he dribbles.

How did the ping-pong players get to shore after the shipwreck?

They paddled!

Why did the runner wear wavy-soled shoes?

To give the ants a fifty-fifty chance.

What did one bowling ball say to the other?

Don't stop me, I'm on a roll.

What's a ghost's favorite position in soccer?

Ghoul-keeper.

What happens when baseball players get old?

They go batty.

Why were the arrows nervous?

Because they were all in a quiver.

What do you get when you cross a football player with a gorilla?

I don't know, but nobody tries to stop it from scoring.

Why did all the bowling pins go down?

Because they were on strike.

Why do soccer players have so much trouble eating?

They think they can't use their hands.

Why was the centipede two hours late for the soccer match?

It took him two hours to put his shoes on.

Why are basketball players always so cool?

Because of all the fans.

Why was the chickens' soccer match a bad idea?

Because there were too many fowls.

GO..GO..GO..THE FREE-RANGE HENS.

Why is tennis such a noisy game?

Because everyone raises a racket.

Why is Cinderella so bad at sports?

Because she has a pumpkin for a coach, and she runs away from the ball.

COMPUTERS

Why was the computer so tired when it got home?

Because . . . it had a hard drive!

Where are computers kept at school?

On their desk drive.

What did the computer say when a man typed something on the keyboard?

You're really pushing my buttons, little man!

How many programmers does it take to screw in a light bulb?

None, it's a hardware problem!

Where do you find the biggest spider?

On the World Wide Web.

Why did the computer cross the road?

Because it was programmed by the chicken.

Why was the robot such a good listener?

He was all gears!

Hey, did you see who stole my computer?

Yes, he went data way!

Why did the computer sneeze?

It had a virus.

What did the computer say to the programmer at lunchtime?

Can I have a byte?

What do computers do when they get hungry?

They eat chips.

What is the computer's favorite dance?

Disk-o.

. . . a man who likes to work out?

Jim!

. . . a girl with a tennis racket on her head?

Annette!

. . . a woman with a cat on her head?

Kitty!

. . . a funny owl?

A hoot!

. . . a boy hanging on the wall?

Art!

. . . a man with a map on his head?

Miles!

. . . a man with a car on his head?

Jack!

. . . a man who owes money?

Bill!

. . . a man with a spade?

Doug!

. . . a man without a spade?

Douglas!

. . . a girl with a frog on her head?

Lily!

. . . a man in a pile of leaves?

Russell!

. . . a woman in the distance?

Dot!

... a man with a Christmas tree on his head?

Noel.

... a woman with a Christmas tree on her head?

Carol.

... a well-read maggot?

A bookworm!

... a man with rabbits in his trousers?

Warren.

Silly BOOK TITLES

How do you do?

Totally Gripping by Paige Turner.

How to Be Taller by Stan Dupp.

A Terrible Nightmare by Gladys Over.

Famous Frights by Terry Fied.

Strong Winds by Gail Forse.

Swimming the English Channel by Frances Neer.

World Atlas by Joe Graffie.

Speaking French by Lorna Lang Wedge.

Close Shaves by Ray Zerr.

Great Eggspectations by Charles Chickens.

How to be Shorter by Neil Down.

Rice Growing by Paddy Field.

Horror Stories by R. U. Scared.

Up the Amazon by P. Rhana.

The Unknown Author by Anne Onymous.

The Long Walk to School by Mr. Bus.

Infectious Diseases by Willie Catchit.

Exercise At Home by Ben Dan Stretch.

A Bullfighter's Life by Matt Adore.

Broken Window by Eva Brick.

The Mad Cat by Claud Boddy.

Egyptian Mummies by
M. Barmer.

Hungry Dog by
Nora Bone.

A Hole in the Bucket by
Lee King.

Camping in Iceland by
I. C. Blast.

The Poltergeist by Eve
L. Spirit.

A Ghost in the Attic by Howie Wales.

Explosives for Beginners by Dinah Might.

Ghosts and Ghouls by Sue Pernatural.

The Omen by B. Warned.

Famous People by Hugh Did-Watt.

Clairvoyance Made Easy by I. C. Ghosts.

Sahara Journey by Rhoda Camel.

Jail Break by Freida Prizner.

The Arctic Ocean by
I. C. Waters.

The Haunted House by Hugo First.

Stormy Day by
A. Pauline Weather.

Dealing With Bullies by
Howard U. Lykett.

The Millionaire by
Iva Fortune.

Easy Money by Robin Banks.

Roof Repairs by Lee King.

A Sting in the Tale by
B. Keeper.

The Rainforest by
Teresa Green.

Across the African Plains
by Ann T. Lope.

Quick Snacks by
Roland Butter.

Crossing Roads Safely by
Luke Bothways.

What happened to the wooden car with wooden wheels and a wooden engine?

It wooden go.

What did the traffic light say to the car?

Don't look now, I'm changing.

What flies and wobbles?

A jellycopter.

Why can't a bicycle stand up?

Because it's two-tired.

When is a car not a car?

When it turns into a garage.

What's a Fjord?

A Norwegian car.

What do you give a sick car?

A fuel injection.

How can you find a lost train?

Follow its tracks.

Policeman: Did you know that you were driving at 120 mph?

Driver: Impossible. I've only been in the car for five minutes.

What kind of car did Elvis drive?

A Rock-n-Rolls Royce.

What do you call an expensive car with a cheap name?

A poor-sche.